You Might Be A Preacher if...

A laugh-a-page look at the life of a preacher.

by Stan Toler

D0972807

Albury Publishing
P.O. Box 470406
Tulsa, Oklahoma 74147

Special Thanks

Special thanks to Terry Toler for creative suggestions and for being our brother. (We love you man!)

Additional thanks to Mechelle Fain for her help in this project.

You Might Be A Preacher If...
ISBN 1-88008-946-7
Copyright © 1995 by Stan Toler & Mark Hollingsworth
P.O. Box 950
Bethany, Oklahoma 73008

Illustrated by Cory Edwards

Published by ALBURY PUBLISHING
2448 East Lewis Street, Suite 4700
Tulsa, Oklahoma 74137

Introduction

Stan Toler and Mark (Toler) Hollingworth are "preacher" brothers. When they get together it's a laugh a minute. Add their preacher brother Terry, and you get triple fun! You Might Be A Preacher If... is an outgrowth of their Monday morning coffee time that is usually spent reviewing and finding the humor in the previous Sunday!

Special Dedication

This book is dedicated to John Minisker, a great church leader and ministry model to all preachers. And to Dr. Melvin Maxwell, the great preaching influence on our lives.

You may be a small town preacher if... After 15 years at your church the other area preachers call you "That new preacher at First and Main."

You hesitate to tell people what you do for a living.

You've ever wanted to speak on commitment but wavered.

Your wife plays the piano.

You drive a "Conversion" van.

Your two car garage sometimes doubles as a Sunday School classroom.

You've ever received an anonymous "U-Haul" Gift Certificate.

You've ever waded in a creek wearing a neck-tie.

You've ever fantasized about "re-baptizing" a deacon.

You've ever been tempted to stock the baptistery with catfish.

You worry about being H.C. (hermeneutically correct).

You've ever dreamed you were preaching only to awaken and discover you were.

You may be a large church preacher if...
You've ever considered a drive-thru counseling center.

You've ever asked for the clergy discount at a garage sale.

You've ever wondered why people couldn't die at more appropriate times.

You find yourself counting people at a sporting event.

People leave while you're talking.

You're leading the church into the 21st century, but don't know what you're preaching on Sunday.

A church picnic is no picnic.

You'd rather negotiate with a terrorist than the church organist.

You jiggle all the commode handles at the church before you leave.

...—●◉●—...

You have a key ring that's bigger than the Junior High School custodian's.

If there really isn't anything new under the sun.

You've ever *wanted* to punch a time clock.

You've ever spoken for free and were worth every penny of it.

···——◉◉——···

You drive a Buick with over 100,000 miles on it.

You might be a "Green" preacher if... You believed your bible school instructor who told you to expect a $40,000 salary your first year.

You've ever wanted to wish people a "Merry Christmas" at Easter 'cause that's the next time you'll see them.

You've ever wanted to punch a board member.

You know the difference between a pharmacist smock and a missionary shirt.

You've ever wanted to fire the church and form a congregation search committee.

You've ever felt like an operator for directory assistance.

You thought that 4-H stood for hose, hair, hem line, and hellevision.

You've ever been tempted to put coupons in the local paper to compete with the Baptists.

You may be a small church preacher if...A quartet and congregational singing are synonymous.

People sleep while you're talking.

If "daycare" and "lawsuit" are synonymous terms.

You've ever been asked to lead the prayer at a High School football game.

It's Sunday but Monday's coming.

Taking a nap on Sunday afternoon is a spiritual experience.

You feel guilty when you go fishing.

You've ever wished you could turn grape juice stains into water stains.

You may be a naive preacher if... You believe the honeymoon will last longer at this new church.

···➤◉➤···

You've ever been asked where to "plug in" the Amplified Bible.

You've learned never to shake
hands with people who seem
to be sitting unusually high
in the hospital bed.

You've ever been asked to do the invocation at a hog-callin' contest.

You can pronounce names like Jeshishai, Mephibosheth, and Quirinius.

You've secretly wanted the worship team to drench you with "Gatorade" after a particularly good sermon.

A denominational executive has ever tried to convince you that Fortuna, North Dakota is the "Land of Opportunity."

$$\cdots\!\!-\!\!\bullet\!\!\circledcirc\!\!\bullet\!\!-\!\!\cdots$$

You wish Tim Conway would do a "Dorf on Preaching" video.

You've ever check your fly as you stood for the opening hymn.

You've seen an ugly bride.

Instead of getting "ticked off" you get "grieved in your spirit."

You may be a large church preacher if...You have baptismal services in the children's wading pool.

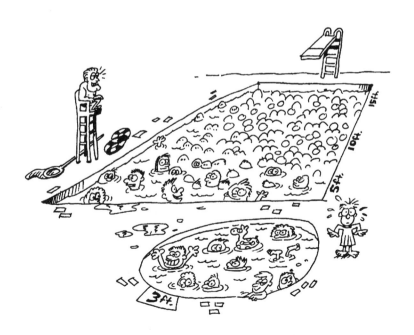

Anyone's ever thanked you for curing their insomnia.

You've ever been asked, "So, what do you do the rest of the week?"

You've ever been tempted to take an offering at a family reunion.

You read sermons to your kids at night instead of bedtime stories.

You've ever asked the Lord to show you a passage to go to with a great illustration.

Your collar covers a multitude of chins.

You might be a "Green" preacher if...You are shocked to find everyone doesn't give at least 10%.

···——◉——···

You have a bumper sticker that says, "If you love Jesus, don't honk...Tithe!"

Your vacation has ever been interrupted by someone wanting to know where the communion wafers are.

Your job description includes scraping pigeon droppings off the steeple.

You scan the help-wanted ads on Monday morning.

You suffer weekly from P.M.S. (Pre-Message Syndrome).

You've ever had the theological shakes at a community Good Friday service.

You've ever wanted to give the sound man a little "feedback" of your own.

You've ever stood by a grave as two drunken veterans attempt to fold the American flag.

Vacation Bible School is no vacation.

"Resisting the devil" and "confronting the church board" are synonymous.

You'd rather talk to people with every head bowed and every eye closed.

Your boss won't give you Sundays off.

You have slides of the Holy Land.

You may be a small church preacher if...Your prayer chain list has less than two phone numbers.

The New Testament really is Greek to you.

A vote on new hymnals causes a church split.

You've ever had to explain that catechism is not a feline medical procedure.

Your "tools of the trade" include a bible, pulpit, and a set of Wilson Irons.

You've ever had a personality conflict with a deacon — you had one, and he didn't.

You might be a "Green" preacher if... You think everyone loves preachers.

You're good at changing diapers.

You've walked up to the counter at Dairy Queen and ordered a "church split."

You've ever substituted Pennzoil for olive oil..

You may be a small town preacher if...You get a live chicken in the offering.

Wrist watch alarms go off while you're talking.

The local undertaker brings you a ham and calendar every year.

You overhear the head deacon praying "Lord, you keep him humble and we'll keep him poor."

You hesitate to call on Sister Longwind to stand and pray.

You've wondered if there will be music directors in heaven.

You might be an insecure preacher
if...You count your congregation
by ears and not noses.

People write grocery lists while you talk.

You know 501C3 is not a new jean style.

You might be a new preacher if...
Your handicap is still over 40.

You may be an old preacher if...
You and John the Baptist
exchanged illustrations.

You only like two kinds of pie —— hot or cold.

You refer to your work as "feeding sheep."

···———◉———···

You enjoy "sheering" sheep from time to time.

You've ever wanted to "lay hands" on a deacon's neck.

You often feel like you're herding mules rather than shepherding sheep.

You might be a small
church preacher if...
The church treasurer has ever
suggested ways you personally
could save the church money.

You've ever wanted to start a support group for church Janitors.

You've had roast for Sunday dinner.

You put out a lot of fires in a day.

You've been roasted at Sunday dinner.

You wear a lot of hats.

Your greatest joys have been in the church.

You'd like to have a TV ministry but can't afford the wigs and makeup for your wife.

Your greatest disappointments have been in the church.

You've ever lost your religion over tables and chairs.

You get paid weekly.

You've seen it all at weddings.

You get paid weakly.

You've seen it all at funerals.

You might be an uneducated preacher
if...You refer to Dakes Annotated
as Dakes "Anointed" Bible.

You have a motor home named "prayer."

You've ever been asked to pray for a soap opera star.

You've ever been asked to pray for a poodle.

9:30am, 10:30am, or 6:00pm mean anything to you.

If you've ever received an anonymous note.

You can count on your phone ringing the minute you sit down for dinner.

Babies cry while you're talking.

You're a very responsible person —— if anything goes wrong, you're probably responsible.

···➤●◉●➤···

Your family provides Job security for the poultry industry.

You're never off on Christmas, Easter or New Years.

Your sermons have a happy ending — everybody's happy when it ends.

You're tired of the agnostic, dyslexic, insomniac joke.

Your kids are very active in church (they can't sit still.)

You're sick of chili suppers and bean dinners.

You've ever preached on television, but you wife made you get down before you broke something.

You've ever attended a convention only to discover 37 other people wearing the same blazer.

You've ever written a letter of resignation on Monday morning.

You exegete in your sleep.

Instead of "pigging out" you "partake of nourishment."

You've ever talked to someone sitting on a bed pan.

You're job is never done.

You've ever wanted to trade brother "Walk the Halls" for a member to be named at a later time.

You may be a small church preacher if...You can't have a church softball team.

Everything you say has three "P's" and a pun.

You work like the devil for the Lord.

"And In Conclusion..."

The words, "And in conclusion" mean absolutely nothing to you.

You might be an uneducated preacher if...You think King James Version *is* the original manuscript.

You've stopped "havin' a blast" and began "experiencing blessings."

You've never been ashamed of the Gospel, but occasionally have been of your church.

You get amused at people fussin' over the color of carpet.

You play the numbers game but not the lottery.

You've ever wondered what the architect was thinking when he designed the baptismal robing room.

You've ever "beseeched" anyone.

Children doodle while you're talking.

Calamine lotion won't cure your preacher's itch.

You exercise "religiously."

It's your job to comfort
the afflicted and afflict
the comfortable.

You've wanted to tell your secretary who's the boss.

But you're for sure a preacher when...You would live your life over again and do the same things: face the same struggles, study your brains out, and work 1000 hours a week —— all for half the pay and recognition you now get —— that's when you know for sure you're a preacher.

About The Author

Dr. Stan Toler currently serves as Pastor-in-Residence at Southern Nazarene University in Bethany, Oklahoma, and is Vice President of INJOY Ministries located in San Diego, California. Stan has touched hundreds of lives with his INJOY "Model Church Seminars" and is widely known as a "Pastor to Pastors."

Prior to accepting the position at Southern Nazarene University, Stan served as Senior Pastor in four growing Nazarene churches across the United States. His most recent assignment was at the historic 2,000 member First Church of the Nazarene located in Nashville, Tennessee. Prior to his 26 years of pastoral experience Dr. Toler served at Circleville Bible College and Florida Beacon as Professor of Homiletics, Systematic Theology, and Greek.

Other published works and manuals
by Dr. Toler include:

Essentials to Evangelism
75 Years of Powerful Preaching
Proven Principles of Stewardship
Lessons for Growing Christians
A History of the Oklahoma City First Church of the Nazarene
Church Empowerment Manual
Minister's Little Instruction Book
ABC's of Evangelism
104 Sermons —— Co-Authored with John Maxwell
Pastor's Guide to Celebrations and Events
Team Building

For Speaking Engagements contact

Stan Toler
P.O. Box 950
Bethany Oklahoma, 73008